Nice Tourist Guide

Attractions, Eating, Drinking, Shopping & Places To Stay

Stacy Lees

Copyright © 2015, Astute Press
All Rights Reserved.

No part of this publication may be reproduced, stored in a retrieval system, or transmitted, in any form or by any means without the prior written permission of the publisher, nor be otherwise circulated in any form of binding or cover other than that in which it is published and without similar condition being imposed on the subsequent purchaser.

If there are any errors or omissions in copyright acknowledgements the publisher will be pleased to insert the appropriate acknowledgement in any subsequent printing of this publication.

Although we have taken all reasonable care in researching this book we make no warranty about the accuracy or completeness of its content and disclaim all liability arising from its use.

Table of Contents

Welcome to Nice 6
Culture 7
Orientation 9
When to Visit 10
Recommended Sightseeing & Activities 12
    Old Town (Vieux Nice) 12
    Palais Lascaris 14
    Place Massena 15
    Palais Massena 16
    Russian Cathedral 16
    Promenade des Anglais 17
    Promenade du Paillon 18
    Castle Hill 18
    Phoenix Flora Park 19
    Musee Matisse 20
    Musee National Marc Chagall 21
    Cimiez Convent (Monastere de Cimiez) 22
    Roman Ruins at Cimiez 23
    Cote d'Azur Observatory 24
    Saint Jean Cap-Ferrat 25
    Villa & Jardins Ephrussi de Rothschild 25
    Train des Pignets 26
Recommended Budget Accommodation 28
    Hotel d'Ostende 28
    Hotel Trocadero 29
    Hotel Rossetti 30
    Anis Hotel 30
    Villa Saint Exupery Garden & Beach 31
Recommended Budget Dining 32
    Le Lodge Restaurant 32
    Chez Papa Fred Restaurant 33
    Lou Pilha Leva Restaurant 33
    Le Maquis Restaurant 34

Cafe Gecko Restaurant..34
Recommended Shopping..35
Cours Saleya Flower Market 35
Boutique Fragonard..36
Maison Auer 37
Hit Import...37
Other Shopping Highlights...38

NICE TOURIST GUIDE

Welcome to Nice

The most recognisable view of Nice in the South of France is its sweeping Promenade des Anglais lined with palm trees and set against the idyllic backdrop of the azure blue Mediterranean Sea. As the largest city on the French Riviera (Côte d'Azur), Nice has been a popular destination for the jet set of Europe for more than 125 years. Visitors and residents include royalty, world-famous artists, award-winning authors and A-list actors. It is one of *the* places to see and be seen.

Nice is located only 20 km from Monaco, which can easily be visited on a day trip. You can travel to nearby Antibes to visit the Picasso Museum or view the largest yacht in the world. Equally convenient is its proximity to Cannes and St Tropez and for a change of scenery, consider exploring the lavender fields of Provence or skiing the snowy slopes of the French Alps.

The city has much to offer in its own right. You can enjoy a large selection of watersports and land-based activities such as surfing, canoeing, scuba-diving and cycling. The famous Promenade des Anglais offers you the choice of roller-blading, skateboarding or enjoying a leisurely stroll in the sun. Sunbathers can spend some time soaking up the sunshine on one of the 22 beaches in and around Nice.

Art lovers will like the city's many galleries and may wish to see the museums devoted to the art of Henri Matisse and Marc Chagall. The city also has a specialist museum featuring a large collection of rare musical instruments. Fashionistas will find themselves in paradise, with so many trendy shopping outlets to choose from and history lovers may wish to sink their teeth into the city's multi-layered history, which goes back thousands of years to the cultures of ancient Greece and Rome.

Culture

The area around Nice has been inhabited since prehistoric times, as a nearby archaeological site at Terra Amata confirms in finds of up to 380,000 years old. Later, it was settled around the 4th century BC by Greeks, before being assimilated into the Roman Empire. Until 1860, it was part of Italy.

From the mid-19th century, with the advent of rail, the city became a popular holiday destination for Russian and English aristocrats and other wealthy travellers.

Queen Victoria was a regular at the Regina Hotel in Cimiez and other famous residents and visitors included the Russian playwright Anton Chekhov, philosopher, Frederick Nietzsche, the American author F. Scott Fitzgerald, the artists Henri Matisse and Raoul Dufy and the actress Isadora Duncan, whose tragic car accident took place in the streets of Nice.

Nice is a small city, with a relatively provincial character and it retains Italian and Corsican influences from its past. Tourism plays a huge role in the local economy. Some of the citizens still speak Niçard, an old local dialect, which is related to Provençal, but most of the current residents of Nice speak only French or are bilingual. "Nissa la Bella", an unofficial anthem of Nice is in Niçard. Street signs in the Old Town section of Nice are also given in French and Niçard.

Some of the regional dishes of Nice include Petits Pissaladieres, a type of savoury tartlet with anchovies and onions as filling, Salad Nicoise, Ratatouille and Pan Bagnat, a tuna and vegetable sandwich.

There is a full calendar of cultural activities in the city. Nice holds an annual 15-day carnival (http://www.nicecarnaval.com/) during the second half of February, which features international entertainers, colorful parades and flower battles. The tradition goes back centuries. In July, the Nice Jazz Festival takes place, as well as the Pink Parade. The city also has a number of art galleries and many of its buildings feature an interesting blending of Baroque, Belle Epoque and Modernist influences.

Orientation

Nice is located on the southeastern coastline of the Mediterranean Sea on the Côte d'Azur also known as the French Riviera. It is located about halfway between Cannes and Monaco and is the fifth most populous city of France, with a population of just over a million. After Paris, it is the French city with the largest concentration of hotels and its airport is the busiest, after Paris Charles de Gaulle and Paris Orly. It is the capital of the Alpes-Maritimes region.

There is a well-connected rail service in the French Riviera, which links Nice to other nearby towns and cities such as Cannes, Grasse, Mandelieu, Marseilles and Toulon as well as Ventimiglia and Cuneo in Italy. A train ticket to Monaco costs just €7. If you plan to do a little exploring, consider obtaining the Carte Azur, a travel card that allows for unlimited travel in the surroundings of Nice.

A great way to explore the city is through the open top hop-on, hop-off bus, which provides audio commentary along the route and stops at fourteen of the main tourist attractions. Ligne d'Azur operates a network of over 40 bus and tram routes around Nice. There is also a well connected bus and tram system.

You may consider doing your own driving, especially if you plan to explore the countryside. The main highway from Toulon to Menton, is a toll road, namely the A8. The fare from Cannes to Nice is €2.90. French toll roads operate on a pay-as-you-go system. Parking can also be quite a problem, with free parking in Nice being scarce to non-existent. If you plan to do some intensive sightseeing in a short time, consider a French Riviera pass, that will allow you unlimited access to all the tourist sites and museums in and around Nice.

When to Visit

One of the greatest attractions of Nice is its sunny weather. On average, the city will see up to 300 days of sunshine annually. The hottest months in Nice are July and August, when average day temperatures around 28 degrees Celsius and night temperatures of 20 degrees Celsius can be expected. July is also the driest month in Nice. May, June, September and October still sees day temperatures of 20 and over. In June you can expect the mercury to settle between 25 and 18 degrees Celsius, whereas September experiences day temperatures of 25 degrees Celsius and night temperatures of 17 degrees Celsius. October typically enjoys days around 20 degrees Celsius and nights around 13.2 degrees Celsius.

On average, October experiences the highest rainfall figures. In May, you can expect average temperatures between 21 and 14 degrees Celsius, while April sees day temperatures around 17 degrees Celsius and night temperatures of around 10 degrees Celsius.

Winters in Nice are still quite sunny, but temperatures could go as low as 10 degrees Celsius. The coldest months are December, January and February, which typically sees temperatures between 12.5 and 13.5 degrees Celsius by day and 4.9 and 5.7 degrees Celsius at night. Towards the end of winter, though, Nice brings out its colorful party clothes for the Nice Carnival, which might appeal to some visitors. The spring months from March to May are a popular time to visit, as is September and October. The peak holiday season is from the end of May to the end of August.

Recommended Sightseeing & Activities

Old Town (Vieux Nice)

Vieux Nice, 06000
Nice, France (Centre)

After the beaches and the Promenade, one of the most intriguing parts of Nice is its historical Old Town section, also known as Vieux Nice.

The streets are narrow and full of character and it is here that Nice is at its most vibrant by day and by night. Take a few hours to stroll around and enjoy the Baroque architecture, the lively markets such as the Cours Saleya Flower market and the many galleries.

At the heart of the Old Town is Place Rossetti, an attractive square flanked by various restaurants. Its most visually prominent features are the fountain and the Cathedrale Sainte-Reparate. The cathedral was constructed between 1650 and 1699 to replace an earlier building which dates back to the 13th century. A bell tower was added during the 18th century and the Baroque facade dates back to the 19th century. There are three organs, as well as ten chapels dedicated to various saints, including Saint Reparata, who is also honored in the artwork of the altar and whose remains are housed within the cathedral.

Giuseppe Garibaldi was a prominent figure in Italian history and at the time of his birth, Nice was still part of Italy. The charming little Old Town square known as Place Garibaldi, features as its centerpiece a statue honoring its namesake. The square was designed by Antoine Spinelli. It is flanked by various Baroque style buildings and the monument itself incorporates a beautiful fountain. There are various cafes nearby that sell refreshments or ice cream.

One of the most prominent buildings on Place Saint-Francois is the Palais Communal or former Town Hall.

The original structure dates back to the 16th century, but various embellishments, such as a new facade, were added in the 18th century. Other features are the bell tower and the Dolphin Fountain at the center of the square.

Palais Lascaris

15 rue Droite, 06300
Nice, France (Old Town / Vieux Nice)
Tel: +33 4 93 62 72 40

Palais Lascaris is the largest civil building of Baroque design in the Old Town section of Nice. It was built during the early part of the 17th century and remained in the Vintimille-Lascaris family until 1802. There are various interesting decorative features, such as a large staircase with elaborate frescoes as well as frescoed ceilings and stucco ornaments. The general theme of the decor borrows heavily from Greek myth. The palace has been furnished with a selection of antique furniture from the 17th and 18th century and Aubusson tapestries. Palais Lascaris was acquired by the city of Nice in 1942 and subsequently restored from 1962. In 1970, it first opened to the public.

The palace houses an important collection of musical instruments that the city acquired from a bequest by Antoine Gautier.

Among the exhibits, visitors will find the oldest trombone in the world, a selection of rare early Baroque guitars from the 17th century, a famous guitar by Antonio de Torres, several harps, including an early harp by the French instrument maker Sébastien Érard, several instruments by Adolphe Sax, the inventor of the saxophone, several violas, violins, recorders and a harpsichord from the 18th century. There is a display of rare clarinets, about 50 non European instruments and several experimental instruments. Admission is free.

Place Massena

Place Massena, 06000 Nice, France (Centre)

The largest and best known of the Old Town's squares is Place Massena, which lies at the heart of Nice and links the historical Old Town with Boulevard Jean-Medecin. One unusual feature of Place Massena is the presence of a collection of illuminated statues. There are seven figures, sometimes likened to philosophers, who perch on seven columns above a stylized layout of chequered flagstones. These statues symbolically represent the seven continents and the communication between different cultures and communities. They were designed by the Spanish artist Jaume Plensa and light up in different colors at night.

Equally impressive is the Fontaine du Soleil, which features a statue of the god Apollo as centerpiece, surrounded by five bronze figures representing Earth, Mars, Venus, Saturn and Mercury.

There is an antique market on Mondays and the square is surrounded by various shops and street cafes. It sometimes provides a venue for outdoor concerts and is used for the Nice carnival. There is a tram station just off the square and only a few minutes away you will find Promenade de Anglais. As a popular meeting place, it is usually buzzing with activity.

Palais Massena

65 Rue de France,
06000 Nice, France
Tel: +33 4 93 91 19 10

This beautiful Belle Epoque villa was built between 1898 and 1901 by Victor Massena , Prince of Essling and Duke of Rivoli. Around 1919, ownership was transferred to the city of Nice and in 1975, the building was listed as a historical monument.

Nowadays, Palais Massena houses the collection of the Museum of History and Art. There are over 15,000 individual exhibits and these include Impressionist paintings from the School of Nice, artefacts of the Napoleonic period, posters from the Belle Epoque era, Empire Style furniture, ceramics and French folk art. It is surrounded by a fragrant garden that offers beautiful views of the Promenade des Anglais. Admission is free.

Russian Cathedral

Av Nicolas II,
06000 Nice, France
Tel: 06 78 05 04 55
http://www.cathedrale-russe-nice.fr/

With its six golden cupola, the Russian Cathedral is largest Russian Orthodox church in Western Europe. Its construction was funded by Tsar Nicholas II and building was completed in 1912, just before the Russian Revolution.

The Russian Cathedral houses a large collection of icons and features exceptional decorative woodwork and frescoes. The church was dedicated to Nicholas Alexandrovich, Tsarevich of Russia, who died in Nice in 1865. Admission is €3. (At the time of writing, the cathedral was closed for an extended period to accommodate renovations.)

Promenade des Anglais

Promenade des Anglais, also known as the Promenade, goes back to the time when the city played host to aristocrats from England and Russia. This broad walkway hugs the coastline for several kilometers and is lined with restaurants, bars, hotels and luxurious Italian style houses. There is a special lane for cyclists and the route is popular with rollerbladers, skate-boarders and strollers.

A recent addition is the Quai Rauba Capeu, which links the Promenade to the Port. At this location, you can admire a rather unusual sundial or pay homage to the city's war casualties at the Monument to the Dead.

If you enjoy a regular courtship with Lady Luck, you may wish to stop off at Casino Ruhl, which boasts 300 slot machines and the facilities for a variety of other games of chance. The casino also has a bar, restaurant and cabaret venue. If you appreciate Art Deco, you may enjoy a closer look at two fine examples of this style of architecture - the Hotel Negresco and Hotel Le Palais de la Mediterranee.

Promenade du Paillon

City Center, Nice

Promenade du Paillon was newly inaugurated after an extravagant renovation process in 2013. The area now features a striking collection of electronically controlled fountain jets and a splash area for kids. This is also a free Wi-Fi zone. Bordering Promenade du Paillon you will find attractions such as the National Theatre of Nice, the Museum of Modern and Contemporary Art, Lycée Massena and Place Garibaldi.

Castle Hill

Castle Hill was originally the site of an fortified citadel. The castle is no more, but today it encompasses a park with a beautiful man-made waterfall that offers amazing views of Nice and the azure sea below.

There are Roman ruins, as well as a play area for children, a few souvenir shops and a snack shop. Visitors who do not mind a little climbing, can follow routes from Place Garibaldi or Promenade des Anglais. If you are a little less active, you could take the Petit Train or get aboard the free lift from the Promenade.

Phoenix Flora Park

405 Promenade des Anglais
(by the airport)
Tel: (33) 0493 180 333
http://www.parc-phoenix.org/

One of the best places in Nice for nature lovers is Parc Phoenix, a 7 hectare botanical garden which houses over 2500 different plant species. Among its attractions are 20 themed gardens as well as a musical fountain, which plays a repertoire of popular classical pieces such as the Tales of Offenbach and well-known Viennese waltzes. The large lake is home to a variety of bird species such as ducks, black swans and pelicans.

A highlight of the park is its diamond shaped greenhouse, the largest of its kind in Europe, which accommodates plant species from seven different climate zones. There is a special section dedicated to orchids. The facility is home to a number of exotic animals such as spiders, iguanas, caymen, flamingos and ostriches as well as a beautiful variety of free roaming butterflies. Visit the aviary for a closer look at nine different raptors and a number of vividly colored parrots and other bird species.

Parc Phoenix welcomes around half a million visitors per year. There is a play area for children, which includes an innovative bamboo maze and dedicated picnic sites. It is located near the airport. Admission of €2 is charged.

Musee Matisse

164 ave des Arenes de Cimiez,
06000 Nice, France (Cimiez)
Tel: (+33) (0)4 93 81 08 08
http://www.musee-matisse-nice.org/

The artist Henri Matisse lived and worked in Nice for over three decades. He was a pioneer of the style now known as Fauvism and can be regarded as one of the most significant French artists of the 20th century. His work was characterized a vivid use of bright color. In 1952, towards the end of his life, he established Musee Matisse.

The museum is housed in a 17th century villa originally known as Gubernatis Palace and at first, the building was shared with the Museum of Archaeology. It now has the third largest collection of Matisse works in France. The earliest works were donated by the artist himself and later pieces were contributed by his wife and members of his family. Besides 68 paintings, it also includes 57 sculptures, lithographs, paper cut-outs, piscine tiles, silk screen prints and illustrated books. There are also photographs of the artist at work and personal possessions such as ceramics, tapestries, stained glass and personal documents. The gift shop sells books and cards. Admission is free.

Musee National Marc Chagall

Avenue du Docteur Menard,
06000 Nice, France
Tel: 04 93 53 87 20

Picasso described Marc Chagall as the only artist besides Matisse who understood what color is. Chagall was born in what is now Belarus, but spent periods of his life in France and the USA, absorbing the influences of Cubism and Fauvism and reflecting it in his own vivid and lively portrayals of Jewish culture and circus performers, as well as images related to fantasy.

The Musee National Marc Chagall is located on Cimiez Hill and houses the largest permanent collection of his works. These include a number large paintings focussing on scenes from the Old Testament. The stories of Genesis and the Exodus feature prominently, but there is also a striking painting of Elijah with the fiery chariot, as well as a series themed around Song of Songs. Two spectacular stained glass windows and a mosaic above the garden pond were specifically created for the museum. The mosaic is a replica of the rose window at Metz Cathedral. Most of the works were donated by Chagall or his wife Valentina and there is also a video presentation detailing the highlights of his life and career. Admission is € 7.50.

Cimiez Convent (Monastere de Cimiez)

Place Jean Paul II,
06000 Nice, France
Tel: 0033 04 9381 0040

Another spot on the itinerary of visitors to Nice, is Cimiez Convent, a timeless place of peace and seclusion. The monastery was founded in the 9th century by Benedictines, but occupation shifted to the Franciscan Order from the 13th century. The complex still has a small community of Franciscan friars as well as a Franciscan museum that provides valuable insight into the daily lives of Franciscan monks throughout the centuries. Individual objects, such as the ancient sundial serve to enlighten modern visitors about the rhythms of a devotional institution. There are several works by the local religious artist Louis Brea in the monastery, such as the Pieta, completed in 1475, the Crucifixion and the Deposition from the Cross.

In the cemetery, you can pay your respects to the graves of Henri Matisse, the artist Raoul Dufy and the Nobel Prize winning author Roger Martin du Gard. The garden is tranquil and beautiful and allows stunning views of the city of Nice. There is a large olive grove. The entire complex has been listed as a historical monument. Admission is free.

Roman Ruins at Cimiez

The neighborhood of Cimiez lies over the foundations of a Roman settlement known as Cemenelum. Visible reminders of this legacy can be found in ruins of Roman baths, in the remains of a paved East-West road and an amphitheatre. In its original incarnation, the amphitheater had been a modest structure of wood that could only accommodate between 500 and 600 spectators. Between 193 and 217 AD, the facility was upgraded to a construction of stone with a capacity to seat up to 5000 spectators. It is sometimes used for live events, including the annual Nice Jazz Festival.

The complex of Roman baths at Cimiez is the largest known facility of its kind in France. Its amenities included a cold bath, warm bath, hot bath, sweat bath and swimming pool. There was also a courtyard and an exercise area. It has been theorized that the West baths might have been a women's section, since a significant concentration of hairpins and earrings have been uncovered from its drainage system.

Right next to the site of the amphitheater is the Archaeological museum and here, some of the artefacts excavated from the amphitheater as well as the baths can be viewed. There are two floors filled with Roman relics. These include jewellery, coins and statues. There is also an altar that incorporates carved relief work of the rooster and the caduceus, both emblems associated with Mercury, as well as altars that have been linked to Jupiter.

Amongst the other artwork, you can view several bronze figurines of Hercules and a dancing faun. Other Roman objects include tombstones and sarcophagi, of which a 3rd century paleo-Christian sarcophagus is particularly notable. Some of the earliest artefacts on display attest to a pre-Roman connection with Greek culture. Among these are Greek kraters from the 4th to 5th BC that have been decorated with various scenes from myths. The site has an interactive children's area, with fun educational tasks. Admission is free.

Cote d'Azur Observatory

Boulevard de l'Observatoire,
06304 Nice, France
Tel: 04 92 00 30 11
https://www.oca.eu/

Although no longer the cutting edge scientific facility of old, the Observatory of Nice remains of interest for a number of reasons. The building itself was constructed according to the plans of architect Charles Garnier, but its main dome is the work of Gustave Eiffel. You can also view a number of historical instruments used for astronomical study here. Most significant of these was a 77cm refractor telescope designed by Henry and Gautier which was once the largest of its kind at a private observatory. Tours need to be booked in advance.

Cote d'Azur Observatory is located at the summit of Mont Gros and here visitors can enjoy panoramic views of the bay and surroundings. There are also great picnic spots.

Saint Jean Cap-Ferrat

Do you want to see where the beautiful people of yesteryear hung out? Then do make your way to Saint Jean Cap-Ferrat, located halfway between Nice and Monaco, only 25 minutes drive from Nice. Some of the more famous residents have included Charlie Chaplin, David Niven, Elizabeth Taylor, Rainer III of Monaco, King Leopold II of Belgium, Isadora Duncan, Winston Churchill, Somerset Maugham and Andrew Lloyd Webber.

The forested and mostly unspoilt peninsula offers great opportunities for hiking or enjoying water sports such as wake boarding, skiing or snorkelling. Feast your eyes on the spectacular sea views or the sight of the luxurious holiday villas of the wealthy. Relax at Paloma beach or dip into the crystal clear water, but keep your eyes open, as you could just spot a celebrity or two. Villa Santo Sospir might also be worth a visit, as it features interiors decorated by the versatile poet and designer, Jean Cocteau.

Villa & Jardins Ephrussi de Rothschild

Av. Ephrussi, 06230, St-Jean-Cap-Ferrat, France
Tel: +33 (0)4 93 01 33 09
http://www.villa-ephrussi.com/

The highlight of a trip to Saint-Jean Cap-Ferrat has to be visit to the former villa of Beatrice Ephrussi de Rothschild.

It's a wealthy French socialite and art collector. Her villa occupies a prime hillside location with magnificent sea views and is surrounded by nine opulent and well-maintained themed gardens. These include a Florentine garden, Spanish garden, Japanese garden and Provencal garden and among its features, you will be charmed by rare trees, beautifully shaded walking paths, ponds, waterfalls, and musical fountains.

The villa once hosted lively musical soirees and literary gatherings. Nowadays, it houses a wonderful selection of art, especially from the 18th century, exquisitely crafted antique furniture, which includes a writing desk made for Marie-Antoinette, a number of Flemish and Beauvais tapestries and a stunning collection of Sevres and Vincennes porcelain. You can enjoy beautiful views of the views of Bay of Villefranche from the tea room or browse through the cultural gift shop for a selection of books, post cards, ornaments and souvenirs. Admission is €9.50.

Train des Pignets

http://www.trainprovence.com/

The palm lined beaches of the Riviera are easy on the eye, but if you want to take a few hours to explore the hinterland of the Mediterranean, book a ride aboard Train des Pignets.

Starting at Nice, the 151km route to Dign-les-Bains takes about three hours and passes olive groves and impressive gorges to offer majestic views of snow-capped mountains. An interesting stop to make along the way is Entrevaux, with its fortified citadel which dates back to medieval times. Another popular stopover is Annot. Stations are quaint and picturesque. Steam train enthusiasts may wish to inquire about the dates on which older locomotives and carriages are used.

Recommended Budget Accommodation

Hotel d'Ostende

3, rue d'Alsace Lorraine, 06000 Nice, France
Tel: +33 (0)4 93 88 72 48
http://www.hotelostende-nice.com/en/

Hotel d'Ostende might have seen better days, but its central location, near the train and tram stations is very convenient for travellers.

There are several restaurants and shops nearby and the area can be a little noisy at night. Reception is available 24 hours and the staff are friendly and speak English. Rooms are compact, but cosy and comfortable with ensuite bathroom amenities. Only some of the rooms have television and Wi-Fi coverage is available in the common rooms. Accommodation begins at €55 for a single room, €73 for a double, €78 for a twin room and €92 for a triple room.

Hotel Trocadero

7 Rue de Belgique,
6000 Nice, France (Centre)
Tel: +33493882431
http://www.hoteltrocadero.net/en/

Hotel Trocadero can be described as somewhere between an upmarket backpacker's lodge and a budget hotel. One of its advantages is the convenient location right by the Nice-Ville train station which facilitates easy transfers to other parts of the French Riviera, as well as the Principality of Monaco. On the down side, the area can become a little seedy at night.

The beach and tourist areas of Nice is about 15 minutes walk away and there are several restaurants nearby. Rooms are small, but well-maintained and comfortable and include cable TV, ensuite bathroom amenities, a wardrobe and air-conditioning. Reception staff are friendly and speak good English. Free Wi-Fi is available in the common areas of the hotel. Accommodation begins at €56 for a single room, €72 for a double room and €84 for a triple room.

Hotel Rossetti

1 rue Sainte Reparate,
06300 Nice, France (Old Town / Vieux Nice)
Tel: 00 33 4 97 08 13 97
http://www.hotelrossetti.fr/

Hotel Rossetti is located in the pedestrianized zone of the Old Town, only a few meters from Place Rossetti and near restaurants, shops, the flower market and the Promenade. The design is trendy and the terrace overlooks the Cathedral Dome. This vibrant area can get a little noisy at night, though. The staff at the reception desk speak English and can be described as friendly and helpful. All rooms include bathroom amenities, air-conditioning, flat screen TV and free Wi-Fi. Seasonal rates are charged. The most basic room begins at between €75 and €115 per night. Breakfast is €9.

Anis Hotel

50 Avenue De La Lanterne,
06200 Nice, France (Formerly Atel Costa Bella)
http://www.hotel-anis.com/

Anis Hotel is located near Nice airport, a short walk from Promenade des Anglais, but a little further from the city center.

Some guests may find the beautiful hilltop site somewhat physically challenging. There is a swimming pool, restaurant, bar/lounge and business center with internet access. Rooms include satellite TV, a minibar, a safe and air-conditioning. Free Wi-Fi coverage is also available. Some rooms have terraces or sea views. Accommodation begins at €70.

Villa Saint Exupery Garden & Beach

22, Avenue Gravier (Garden)
6 Rue Sacha Guitry (Beach)
Nice, France
Tel: +33 4 93 84 42 83
https://www.villahostels.com/en

Villa Saint Exupery manages two hostels in the city of Nice. The cheaper one, Villa Saint Exupery Garden is located in a converted monastery with private garden. The down side is the fact that this location is a little further from the city center and the beach, but fortunately there is a regular shuttle service. The hostel also has a large modern lounge/bar, a restaurant, communal kitchen and BBQ area, as well as computers and free Wi-Fi access. Secure lockers are available and various fun activities can also be arranged. Dorms range from €26.50 per night, whereas private rooms are available from €31.50 per night. Breakfast is included.

If you can afford a little more, Villa Saint Exupery Beach has a more convenient location in the heart of Nice and near the Old Town and beach area.

There is a bar, a gym and a TV lounge and tours and adventurous excursions can be arranged. Guests can also sign up for the free walking tour of Nice. There are secure lockers and free computer usage and Wi-Fi access. Accommodation at Villa Saint Exupery Beach begins at €41.95 for dorms and €52.50 for private rooms. Breakfast is included.

Recommended Budget Dining

Le Lodge Restaurant

14 rue Halevy,
06000 Nice, France (Centre)
Tel: +33 4 93 88 41 89
http://www.lelodgerestaurant.com/

Le Lodge Restaurant is located in the Carré d'Or area and offers indoor and outdoor seating, with a capacity to accommodate close to 100 people. Diners can enjoy a set three course menu for €21, with choices including dishes such as salmon salad, onion soup, pizza, fillet steak, salmon 3 ways, ravioli ricotta, sea bass and tenderloin beef with vegetables and sautéed potatoes.

Chez Papa Fred Restaurant

25 Boulevard de la Madeleine,
06000 Nice, France
Tel: 0493868460

Although a small restaurant with about twelve tables, Chez Papa Fred will be sure to surprise you with its great food, relaxed atmosphere and friendly service. English is spoken and an English menu is available. Dishes of duck, lamb and steak form the backbone of the menu, but the menu also includes dishes like the warm cheese salad, goose liver salad, ravioli with white truffle sauce, sea bream, turkey escalope with mushroom sauce and salmon with saffron sauce. A highlight of the dessert menu is 'hot and cold' chocolate cake, served with vanilla sauce and vanilla ice cream. There is a set three course dinner charge of €25.

Lou Pilha Leva Restaurant

10 rue du Collet,
Nice, France (Old Town/Vieux Nice)

There are not all that many cheap eateries in Nice, but you can expect a budget meal at Lou Pilha Leva restaurant. It is located in the Vieux Nice or Old Town section and one of the house specialities is socca, a local favorite which can be described as chickpea based flatbread.

Other menu items include pissaladiere, farcis or stuffed vegetables, pizza, salad nicoise, daube pasta and soupe au pistou. The socca is priced at only €2.50 and most of the other items are under €10.

Le Maquis Restaurant

7 Rue de L'abbaye,
06300 Nice, France
Tel: 0493012705

Le Maquis is a cosy restaurant that specializes in Corsican style cuisine. There is a set three course menu offered at €26 and some of the choices you can expect include smoked salmon summer salad, eggplant fritters, foie grass with fig jam, risotto, artichoke salad with mozzarella and cured ham, tuna steak with mashed potatoes, pizza and lamb shank in orange and red wine glaze. Dessert choices include melon salad and Nutella dessert.

Cafe Gecko Restaurant

29 boulevard Raimbaldi, 06000 Nice, France
Tel: +33 9 83 09 09 60
http://www.cafe-gecko.com/

As a small bistro, Cafe Gecko offers friendly service and quick affordable food.

Standard fare on the menu include salads, risotto, burgers, pasta and fish and meat, and some of the more interesting items include fried sweet potato and foie gras sorbet. The gourmet coffee also comes highly recommended. Most menu items are priced at between €4 and €16.

Recommended Shopping

Cours Saleya Flower Market

Est de la rue Droite,
06300 Nice, France
Tel: 33 4 92 14 48 00

The Cours Saleya Flower Market is located in Vieux or Old Nice, just below Castle Hill and has been the main market square of the city of Nice since medieval times. It is the largest flower market on the Riviera, but you can also shop here for seasonal fruit and vegetables and food items like cheese, olives, sausages, cheese, spices and candy. There are plenty of vendors selling snacks and light meals like crepes, pizza slices and even seafood. There are also souvenir items and a large selection of locally made soaps and lavender items.

Bear in mind that Grasse, the Provencal capital of perfume is not too far away. On Mondays the setting changes slightly when the antique traders set up shop. Some of their wares include second hand books and records, paintings, coins, vases and stamps.

You can expect live street entertainment as well. During the peak holiday season, an art and raft market trades here from 6pm til late.

Boutique Fragonard

11 Cours Saleya
06300 - Nice
Tel: +33(0)4 93 80 33 71
http://www.fragonard.com/

The House of Fragonard dates back to 1926 and was named after the artist Jean-Honoré Fragonard by founder Eugène Fuchs. Today, the establishment sells a wide range of perfumes, soaps, cosmetics and other related toiletries. These include scented candles, bath salts, shower gels and a selection of novelty soaps. If you are interested in scent, consider enrolling for a special workshop to educate yourself on the use and creation of fragrances.

The Perfumer's Apprentice workshop allows you to create your own customized eau de toilette. This unique hour and a half experience will teach you everything about the history of perfume and scent recognition. The facilitator will discuss the theory behind the fragrance pyramid and finally assist you in the tailoring of your own unique fragrance. The workshop costs €65 and is available in English or French.

Maison Auer

7 Carriera San-Francès-de-Paula,
06300 Nice, France
Tel: +33 4 93 85 77 98
http://www.maison-auer.com/

Foodies, especially those with a sweet tooth, would be well advised to pay a visit to Maison Auer, which features the award-winning culinary creations of Thierry Auer, master confectioner and chocolatier. Among the wares you will find a selection of candied fruits and chestnuts. There is a popular line of chocolates, which includes fillings like coconut praline, sesame praline, orange peel, lemon ganache, vanilla ganache and rum and raisin. These are available in a variety of boxes as well as mini bars. Other items include jams, pastries and salted caramels.

Hit Import

11 Rue Lépante, 06000 Nice France
Tel: +33 4 93 62 38 54
http://www.hitimport.com/

Fans of classic rock music or any of its related genres would be thrilled to browse through the wide selection of CDs at Hit Import.

The staff members are super-knowledgeable and whether you are looking for Goth, techno, death metal or 60 psychedelic music, they should able to unearth some classic rarities at bargain prices. Sample your favorites before you buy. You can also organize concert tickets through this outlet.

Other Shopping Highlights

Nice has a number of fashion stores and if you are serious about shopping, you would probably want to know about the twice-annual sales in January and July. There is an outlet of Galleries Lafayette, one of the largest French department stores near Place Massena. If you are looking for high end fashion, jewellery and shoe shops, do stroll through Avenue Jean Medicin. For four levels of shopping opportunities, visit Nice Etoile, a shopping mall located at number 30 which has outlets for FNAC and Habitat. Nearby is a branch of Monoprix, another well-known French retail store that sells groceries, household items, clothing and gifts. Avenue Jean Medicin also has branches of Zara and H&M. A tram service runs all along the Avenue.

An equally popular street for shoppers is the pedestrianized Rue de France, where you will find plenty of souvenir shops. If you are looking for art, explore Rue Droite. For specialized spice shops and olive products, browse through Rue Pairolière. For shoes and clothing, try your luck on Rue de la Liberte.

NICE TOURIST GUIDE

Printed in Great Britain
by Amazon.co.uk, Ltd.,
Marston Gate.